FLAMING TIMBERS

Rekindling The Heart

Author: Fletcher Johnson Jr.

Publisher:

PIERCING FOCUS LLC

First printing edition 2019

First Published by *Piercing Focus LLC*

11/02/2019

Book design by Piercing Focus LLC

Map by Piercing Focus LLC

ISBN 978-1-7325238-4-5 (Paperback)

Library of Congress Control Number: 1-7856138241

www.flamingtimbers.com

Publishing Company*: Piercing Focus LLC*

Author*: Fletcher Johnson Jr.*

Editor*: Piercing Focus LLC*

Illustrator*: Piercing Focus LLC*

Dedication

I would like to dedicate this book to the woman of my dreams and wife, Valerie Lynn Johnson, who embodies the essence of beauty, class, dignity, love, Godliness and sophistication. She is my best friend, wife, mother of our children and prayer partner. I could not have achieved or dreamed to go beyond my limits if it had not been for her loyal devotion and support. She has always been the woman of my dreams and long before dating, I still recall drawing a sketch of her prior to our meeting. I knew it was meant to be, the moment I stared into her eyes of love. The sketch was a premonition of our future. I want to thank you for taking the time to stop and become acquainted with me during our early years of meeting in college. I will never forget the egg McMuffins and hash browns that she always treated me to. Your kindness and generosity warmed my heart. She was down to earth and never looked down on anyone. I couldn't wait to see, hear and hold her soft hand as we walked along the college campus. I never felt so ecstatic in my life. I remember attending church with her and spending time watching movies. Today, being married to her more than 32 years, I count each day a blessing. The greatest blessing that we both enjoy is the wonderful creation from God, our children, Jarvis, Christopher and Joshua. We also enjoy the new addition, our beautiful daughter-in-law, Jennifer. I give God all the glory for bringing us together in Holy Matrimony.

CONTENTS

Forward

These questions may prompt you to think, pause and focus on what's important in your marriage or relationship. How many couples remember the beginning of their relationship? Do you remember when you first laid eyes on each other? How did your heart feel? Do you remember the keys to his or her heart? Or, did you lose them?

If you're considering marriage or would like to renew your heart, there are seven keys I would like to share with you. After 32 plus years of marriage, I feel it's my obligation and Christian duty to give support to others as they journey through their relationship. In fact, the song, *Through the Years* by Kenny Rogers is one of my favorite songs of long-term love. I include this song in my playlist for my wedding anniversary or whenever I want to reminisce about my love for my wife. Even before we utter the short, but powerful two-syllables, ***"I do,"*** the history of love begins long before we are ever ready to become married.

As a child, I can recall reciting innocent poems with sing-song beats and sweet stanzas that went much like this: *Roses are red, Violets are blue, Sugar is sweet and So are you*. But, when I met and married the love of my life in my young adulthood, the poem changed and became more serious, morphing into a line that went like this: *Roses are red, Violets are blue, I count each day a blessing that I'm married to you*. To be honest, marriage *is* beautiful but at times, it's no fairy tale. It requires love, commitment, support, care, respect and forgiveness. I wrote this book for individuals who are single, in the beginning stage of courtship, engaged, newlywed, already married, divorced, separated, or widowed. We all need coaching, insight and guidance along life's journey as we continue to grow together on this beautiful planet. Just as a road map or a GPS makes it easier when you are looking for a destination, so does the relational journey—which requires navigational devices in understanding stages, keys and strategies to making relationships successful. Therefore, I cheer you and your significant other on as you both embark on the journey of establishing a healthy and fulfilling relationship.

A Little Humor Goes A Long Way

I love starting out by sharing some humorous moments in relationships that some of you can relate to or seen others experience. Have you ever been to a family gathering and said something humorous about your spouse or significant other that he or she didn't think was funny? It could have been perfectly harmless to you but the joke sure hit a sore spot with them! He or she then stare daggers at you while snarling and feigning with fury. At that point, you become red-faced and begin looking for a magician who can make you disappear. Then, to make matters worse, your loving family and friends who are supposed to have your back become *zombies* and thirsty for blood by inciting violence against you, while saying lines such as, "I *know* you're not going to let him get away with that!" So much for blood being thicker than water! Then, as if wild spectators and fans at a Gladiators arena, your *loving* circle begins chanting, jeering, and mocking you. You know you're in trouble when she moves closer while secretly whispering a word that only you can hear. It reminds you of the whispering warning your mom would give, just before she pounced. Suddenly, you hear aloud, "Well, it's time we be going," while she glances back at you with both eyes gazing into your soul." But before you can breathe a sigh of relief that the embarrassment in front of your family and friends is over, you begin thinking of the World War III that's going to take place when you get home. *Deadman walking. I'm walking the Green Mile*, comes across your mind.

Now, the closer you get to the car, you're thinking should I run for the border or text 911 before getting inside. As you approach the driver's side, she snatches the keys with force and her normally sweet voice becomes otherworldly as she says, "No, I'll drive and get in now." At this point, you're petrified and don't know what she's going to do. She's staring at you with fiery red eyes and her teeth suddenly looks sharp. You're thinking this must be a nightmare and this has got to be a horror movie. A question appears in your mind. Should I ask for my last meal of crispy buttermilk fried chicken? Once inside, she speeds around every curve and corner with occasional stares at you with her head spinning around. When you open your mouth to speak, she yells, "Don't you say a word: I've heard enough from you! Just wait until I get you home!" You're thinking, "It's getting real now. Am I sitting next to my Executioner?" This may just be life or death." A scary thought begins racing through your mind as to how her attack might be carried out. Your nervousness increases.

Now, you approach the driveway of the house and the only opportunity you see to escape is by asking if she could drop you off at the mailbox. By the way, she accelerates into the driveway, you realize she's not buying it. As she enters the garage, you attempt to grab the door handle. You're thinking, *"Should I open the door, roll to safety and yell for the neighbors?"* With the garage door closing, you meekly walk inside the house and start praying, *"Lord, have mercy and come help me."* She gets out hurriedly and angrily goes pass you in the house. You're nervous because you don't want to be surprised. You tiptoe inside hearing *Deadman walking* in your head and she's sitting in a chair in the dark. You can only see a silhouette of her. She tells you to sit down and cross-examines you. You're begging for forgiveness but it's not sinking in. She then asks you the obvious question as if you're on a trivia show. This question is worth 30 points. *Do you know where you're going to sleep tonight? You reply "Yes." And, she asks "Where?" You respond, "On the couch." She then responds, "You're correct and it was the top answer on the board. Do you want to keep playing or pass on embarrassing me in front of our friends?"* You then respond, *"I'll pass."* She replies, *"Good choice because for you it would have been sudden death to keep playing with my feelings."* You both began laughing and suddenly it becomes a moment of light heartedness. You apologize on one knee and ask for forgiveness. She says, *"I forgive you, but I am heading to bed. The couch is for you tonight."* With hugs and kisses, it's all good now. So, you spend the next several weeks, months and maybe years making up for this one incident. You become the gift that keeps on giving. Relationships are real but humorous at times. Some of you that are reading this book can relate. Better yet, you are probably hoping this never happens to you. Couples must learn to love, live, laugh, respect and forgive. Adding humor to your marriage with humorous anecdotes is vital and it keeps the relationship alive. Proverbs 17:22 (KJV) reads: *A merry heart doeth good like a medicine: but a broken spirit drieth the bones.*

An Era of Love, Romance and Proposals

During the 18th Century, Romanticism was a way of life, a trend that made devout followers, of philosophers, poets, and artists around the world. It was an age of emotions when the heart was more sensible than the mind. It was a time of courtship, marriages, and romances were expressed in poetry, literature and art.

During the 1960s, romantic films and music captured the hearts and imaginations of many. During the Doo Wop era, music from the 1950s to 1960s reflected love and romance. Groups like The Flamingos sang "I Only Have Eyes for You," The Orioles--"Crying in the Chapel," The Penguins-- "Earth Angel", Curtis Lee With the Halos –Pretty Little Angel Eyes," The Stereos- I Really Love You" and The Willows--"Church Bells May Ring." This was a time where relationships bloomed into marriages marking what is known as the baby boomer's generation. It also marked the beginning of an increasing number of proposals.

The marriage proposal is one of the grandest moments in modern American History. Growing up, many women are enthralled with how their proposal would be performed: *Maybe he'll take me somewhere romantic— I'll have no clue as to what's happening—he'll get down on one knee with his hand stretched out while displaying a huge diamond ring —we'll start crying—he'll pop the question—we'll immediately say yes. It should be magical.*

Whom to marry is among the most important decisions most people will ever make in their lives, not to be taken lightly. Yet, some have made it into a show, with a prefixed grand finale: *"Yes!"* Others have proposed during games, family gatherings, using airplane banners and board games such as Scrabble. Yet, as for women, it is a lifelong childhood dream to be taken seriously. Many have dreamed of meeting and marrying their Prince Charming, while hearing these words: *As I stare into your sparkling blue eyes, I see blue oceans of love and galaxies of stars beaming with majestic lights of the universe. You are truly the most beautiful Angel on earth and if heaven is anything like you, I am already there. If this is a dream, I pray that I never wake up. The glow on your face and the tender touch of your hands tells me that you are the one for me. That means forever and a lifetime. With my heart in my hand, I* want to ask you, will you marry me? "Yes!" is usually the resounding response that leads to the altar.

***Marriage and divorce** are both common experiences. Research shows that In Western culture, more than 90 percent of people marry by age 50. However, between 40 to 50 percent of married couples in the United States divorce. The divorce rate for successive marriages is even higher.*

The Day I Stared into The Eyes of My Love

Come with me, as I take you on my own personal journey of finding true love. During my early years of college, I can recall the most wonderful day of my life, as I stared into the sparkling eyes of an angel, sitting on a bench, with such grace and poise. I can still remember that moment as I walked by staring into her eyes of love. Upon entering class, I found it difficult to focus because the image of her face kept appearing before me.

After arriving home, I told my mother what I'd witnessed, and she jokingly stated, "Stupid, why didn't you talk to her?" I responded with laughter, "I didn't have a pickup line to use in approaching her because you only took me to church and never taught me to date a girl." What I didn't realize was that my mother was teaching me all along how to treat a woman. I remember going on lunch dates with my mother, shopping trips, cuddling, dancing and supporting her when she was sad and sick. In other words, she taught by example. My mother and I both laughed at my comment. The following day, I decided to take the same route to class, in hopes of seeing my Cinderella again. To my dismay, the bench was empty, and my heart sank. I began walking the campus halls in hopes of finding those eyes of love, much like the Prince did when he searched for the girl that fitted the glass slipper. Before long, the semester passed with no sign of her.

As the school year closed, I gave up the search but couldn't escape the recurring images of her face and eyes. I began sharing my experience with a relative and told him that this girl's face keeps appearing before me. He responded, "Why didn't you at least get her name?" I responded, "I don't know, and I was too shy." Well, as summer approached, I decided to take a course or two. While talking to another student on campus, I observed my Cinderella walking out of the student center building. I approached her and politely introduced myself. I can recall speaking these words inside, "Oh my God, I can't believe it's really her and she's just as beautiful as the first day I saw her. She's truly an *Earth Angel*." I stood paralyzed for a moment and almost became speechless. I thought about the great relationship that my mother and I had. I approached the conversation with natural progression of becoming acquainted and she invited me to her church. I gladly accepted, and this was the beginning of our journey.

We exchanged numbers and began dating. During our relationship, we communicated daily using words and expressions such as "I love you", holding hands, staring into each other's eyes, shopping together, laughing, attending movies, conversating, sharing dreams and concerns. We showed genuine support and often fell asleep while talking on the phone. Finding it more and more difficult to be apart, I knew that we belonged together. The day arrived where I couldn't take it anymore and knelt on one knee. While staring up into her sparkling brown eyes, I asked her to marry me and without hesitation, she accepted by saying "Yes." Today, we have been married for more than 32 years and have three wonderful sons along with a daughter-in-law.

Now, it's your turn. Take a moment to reflect on the beginning of your marriage or relationship. What attracted you to that person? Was it his or her eyes, body, hair, intelligence, social status, occupation, money, family, respect, or, was it love? If you chose social status, occupation or money, you are in it for the wrong reasons. Love is intangible, and its' value is priceless and more valuable than any earthly treasure including diamonds. What would you do if your partner lost social status, occupation or money? Would you remain loyal to support him or her through it? Or would you vanish with everything else? If you chose the latter, let me shed some light on your ominous decision. Love is not material wealth or status; it is more valuable than any earthly treasure.

If your partner became sick with a terminal illness or a debilitating disease that was life altering, what would you do? If you chose to leave, let me provide you with a clearer perspective. How would you want to be treated by the love of your life if you lost it all and became terminally ill? Would you want support or abandonment? Believe me, we all will need help as we continue the track of life.

What about all the millionaires, billionaires and celebrities who are divorcing? They have social status, occupations and money but, some lack committed love. On the other hand, some couples have weathered bankruptcies, loss of family members and occupations and have managed to pull through the tough times by expressing their love and commitment.

Here's the litmus test for you. How committed are you to love your wife, husband or friend as you go through tough times?

When a couple dissect their **"I dos"** with the understanding that it's an unconditional promise, then, they will be able to lean on their vows during times of frustration and stress. When you recall your vows, which part do you think about? **"For richer or poorer"**? **"In sickness and in health"**? Or do you think about the final phrase so many couples say – **"so help me, God"**?

For some, saying traditional vows may feel like a hurried disclaimer or being cross-examined on a witness stand: **i.e. 'so help me, God.'** However, we need to think of vows as meaningful, binding covenant, between more than just you and your spouse but with God.

But what if you regret making those marriage vows? Do you wish you would have waited or met someone differently? Or, would you go back and change the last five, 15 or 30 years of your life?

The good news is your vows still hold the key to this predicament. *"From this day forward…"* four words filled optimism, promise and a future. For those who are starting over and finding it difficult to move forward, remember that a rearview mirror is only designed to allow you to glance back but a windshield provides a wider view for you to focus on the road ahead.

Have you said things you wish you could take back? Have you done things you regret?

Some of you right now may face discouragement and look back on your vows with regret. You don't need to. You can have a new start today... *from this day forward*.

Take a moment and focus on today. Your love affair with each other and the greatest marriage you can imagine, begins now. It might feel like you have too many struggles to work through. You don't. It might feel like the hurt is too great to be repaired. It's not. You may not be confident that you have what it takes. But you do! It all begins at the altar with a Holy matrimony of vows exchanged before God.

Fulfilling Your Vows

As I reflect on my own vows that I made at the altar, I think on the time when my wife first discovered that she had MS (Multiple Sclerosis). I had a choice to make and it was easy because I reflected on my vows at the altar where I made this promise statement, *I, **Fletcher**, do take thee, **Valerie**, to be my wife. To have and to hold, in sickness and in health, for richer or for poorer, and I promise my love to you forevermore*. It has been a pleasure, loving and standing by her all these years.

Your vows are more than a collection of words you say once and then forget. As stated before, they are the point at which your relationship became a covenant between you, your spouse and God.

Our commitment to each other is mirrored in our holy covenant before him. And our commitments are based on decisions. The choices you make each day determines the quality of your marriage. The decisions you make today determine the marriage you will have tomorrow. In the event you have forgotten your wedding vows or thinking of marrying soon, you might want to listen to this one. Here's a script that was read to us during our wedding ceremony.

Vows

Would you please face each other and join hands? (*Symbolizes the beginning of joining as one and cleaving to one another as mentioned in the bible*).

(Groom) _____do you take

_____to be your wife?

Do you promise to love, honor, cherish and protect her, forsaking all others

and holding only to her forevermore?

(*"I do"*)

(Bride) _____do you

take_____ to be your Husband?

Do you promise to love, honor, cherish and protect him, forsaking all others

and holding only to him forevermore?

(*"I do"*)

Vows to Be Repeated

(*you may change these vows or write your own*)

(Groom) I, _____ take thee

_____, to be my wife. To have and

to hold, in sickness and in health, for richer or for poorer, and I promise my love to you forevermore.

(Bride) I, _____ take thee _____ to be my Husband. To have and to hold, in sickness and in health, for richer or for poorer, and I promise my love to you forevermore.

Exchange of Rings

For many couples, the wedding ring is a symbol and a public profession that they are married. It is a sign of a commitment for one another and represents the love, honor and faithfulness that you have for your spouse. It is a sign of love and fidelity of your spouse to you. The circle shape of a wedding ring symbolizes that your love for one another is endless and will last forever. For many the **wedding ring** is worn on the fourth finger of the left hand. This is because the vein in this finger was believed to lead directly to the wearer's heart.

Charge to the Couple

_____ and

_____ as the two of you come

into this marriage uniting you as husband and wife,

and as you this day affirm your faith and love for

one another, I would ask that you always

remember to cherish each other as special and

unique individuals, that you respect the thoughts,

ideas and suggestions of one another. Be able to

forgive, do not hold grudges, and live each day that

you may share it together – as from this day

forward you shall be each other's home, comfort

and refuge, your marriage strengthened by your

love and respect. *"You may now kiss the bride".*

The **wedding kiss** is a symbol of a bride and

groom's love and devotion as well as their respect

for each other.

Remember that vows are not mere words,

but binding promises that must be kept daily in

accordance with biblical scriptures. **Ephesians** 5:25

reads: "For husbands, this means love your wives,

just as Christ loved the church. He gave up his life

for her." **Genesis 2:24 reads:** "Therefore a man

shall leave his father and his mother and hold fast

to his wife, and they shall become one flesh." ... He

who loves his wife loves himself. **Mark 10:9 reads:** "Therefore what God has joined together, let no one separate."

So, when the wedding ceremony is over, guests have gone home, and the limousine drops you off, tuxedos returned, the wedding dress hung up, the cake top is put away, and the honeymoon is over, it's time to put those vows into action.

The Seven Stages of Marriage

Establishing a successful marriage is a lifetime journey. Understanding the various stages of marriage and phases is essential to fulfilling and building a strong foundation for the relationship.

Stage One: Desire

This is the celebratory stage, when passion and powerful desirability tie a couple together and lead to vows. This may last for 3 to 6 months before it dwindles within a year or two. However, this stage of desire is very important in solidifying the relationship. Even if you're marrying at a later age or second time, the intense desirability creates a bond. This level of desirability causes couples to fall head over heels in love with each other. This is where love, respect, emotional romance, care, and trust is established in creating support for the relationship.

Stage Two of Marriage: Reality

In this stage, the honeymoon ends, and reality begins. In the reality stage, you discover your spouse has shortcomings, he or she doesn't know how to cook, separate clothes, fold laundry, wash dishes, make beds, raise or lower the toilet seat, or put the ironing board back into place. Discouragement and early disagreements are the milestones of this difficult, inevitable period, as the two of you make the first steps toward accepting each other for who you truly are in real life.

The mission and challenge? Laying the preparation for an extensive future together is dependent on unconditional love, trust and willingness to change. You'll have to self-assuredly talk and listen intently as you both present your most profound individual needs and desires. This establishes a basis for being accepted, understood and supported throughout the relationship.

Stage Three of Marriage: Conflict

She misses her companions; he misses his exciting toys. She needs to hike and explore; he needs to play weekly sports. She needs to manufacture her profession; he needs to revitalize his vocation. Despite successful couples who master the reality stage with a basis for a joyous, responsible co-habitation, a moment arises when selfishness supersedes the interests of the marriage. Furthermore, when this occurs, be prepared for conflict.

During the conflict phase, both partners feel they are justifiably right, yelling in frustration, "You call this a marriage?!!!" Research has shown that this stage of marriage is inevitable. If not, you can wind up spouse that will spell disaster for your marriage. It is sometimes the nature of the conflict more so than the scope of the conversation, that poses problems. The reason this occurs is that conflicting opinions combined with fury and frustration, leads to conflicting actions that spirals into excessiveness, disrespect, and ultimately, betrayal. This is an ultimate collision course that spells disaster for the marriage.

Stage Four of Marriage: Teamwork

As relationships develop throughout the years, they tend to become more complex. Occupations grow, aspirations mature, homes increase in size, and kids are born. In the teamwork phase, the relationship becomes more like a corporation. Retirement plans are made, college expenses are saved, parenting skills develop, health and fitness awareness increases, and spiritual connections become more important.

Step Five of Marriage: Reunification

With kids, the teamwork stage lasts about 15 to 25 years. The relationship begins to return to a reconciliation phase. The children are all grown, financial stability achieved, careers established, goals achieved, car and homes paid off. The couple's role as a provider and parent seems to change. They return to being romantic, innovators and explorers. The thrill returns and now the travels begin. They tend to enjoy sight-seeing, adventures, cruises and spontaneous romantic evenings.

Step Six of Marriage: Unexpected Crisis

This is the critical stage for all marriages and relationships. The moment you get the news that you're losing your job, the death of a child, sibling, parent or family member or you have been diagnosed with a terminal or debilitating disease – major crisis seems to compound themselves. Now, the marriage is facing an earthquake that can only be sustained through true love and commitment. This is where couples must rely on their faith in each other, God, support and prayers. It's important that couples find time to get away, relax, vacation and laugh together. Accept support and don't deny authentic mentorship as well as support. Don't be afraid to reach out for help and never let pride stop you from expressing your feelings to others that are willing to provide comfort. Trust only those that you know really care about you all as a couple. Not everybody that says they are there for you are truly there. Some are just being *busybodies* while others are gloating over your pain.

Stage Seven of Marriage: Accomplishment

In the accomplishment stage, your marriage and relationship have withstood the test of time. You begin to reap the rewards of retirement, enjoying grandkids, laughing, sharing stories and loving each other as if you just met. You both enjoy reminiscing about the beauty of meeting each other and reflecting on your commitment that endured the test of time. You both begin expressing your deepest appreciation for each other and love to give surprise gifts. You both believe that the best is yet to come, and these are the best days of your life. You both also tend to enjoy serving in the church, community, local boards and making a difference in the lives of others.

The Seven Keys of Marriage

By using the following keys that have benefited me over the last 32 plus years, I feel that you can successfully navigate through these stages with some support. Here is the first of Seven Keys:

Key #1: Love

Love is a key that has two phases **(spoken and demonstrated).** They are dependent on each other.

Phase 1: Spoken Love

- Greet your spouse with words that speak to his or her heart. Here are some phrases that I use daily: Good Morning Beautiful, Darling, Sweets, Queen). When answering the phone, I respond with excitement: "Hello, Beautiful! How are you doing? It's good to hear your voice. *I never leave the phone without saying*, "I love you and look forward to seeing you soon. Goodbye, Beautiful").

Phase 2: Demonstrated Love

- Hugs, kisses, message, gifts, listening, dating, communicating
- As for men, love is usually demonstrated most often in the forms of affection.
- As for women, love is usually demonstrated most often through conversation and emotional support.
- However, both men and women desire both on some occasions. So, a healthy balance is most desirable in any relationship. They both co-exist in one prism to a certain degree depending on the prior experiences of the spouse or significant other. In some cases, if your spouse has a background of family dysfunctionality, abuse and abandonment, their need for both is heightened whereas the other spouse may have come from a background of family stability and support. They may require very little. In this case, you must seek to understand as well as being understood because each of you differ. This could mean the difference in maintaining a healthy

relationship or continuing a dysfunctional generational cycle. So, do your research and see if you both are a good fit. Don't ignore the warning signs. Love is demonstrated by care and respect, not abuse.

Healthy Benefits to love:

-       When in love, you may see stars in your eyes, experience butterflies in your stomach or become weak in the knees. You see falling in love is a feeling like no other. But did you know that being in love has tangible health benefits for both your body and your mind? *"We are social creatures and we do best when we have strong social support systems. Being in love can affect everything from your stress levels to your heart health."*

-       It's fitting that the symbol for love is a heart, given all the heart health benefits of being in love.

-       Being in love tends to decrease our stress response, which can, in turn, lower blood pressure. Studies show strong love, marriage and social ties improve blood pressure, while isolation and being around strangers increases it. The same holds true for heart rate.

-       And if you do have a heart attack, being happily married helps. In a 2015 study, married people had a lower risk of dying in the hospital after a heart attack. They also had shorter hospital stays.

- Those with strong, happy marriages lived longer than unmarried men and women. The opposite is true as well and research shows that unhappy married couples have a shorter life span.

- And there's a growing amount of research showing a higher risk of illness and death in people with low quantity and low quality of social relationships. *"Social isolation is a major risk factor for death from a variety of causes in both genders."*

- *"Positive, close relationships with family members and friends can keep you healthier too."*

- Even something as simple as a hug can help. Most people know hugs can help you feel connected to other people, but did you know they can help prevent sickness? When you feel connected to others, especially through physical touch, you're less prone to experience sickness caused by stress.

-        In one study of more than 400 adults, researchers found that the more often people hugged, the more their chances of getting sick decreased. Hugging may be an indicator of overall social support in a person's life, which also promotes good health. In the same study, the adults who said they have a strong social support system had fewer cold symptoms than those who said their support system was lacking.

-        No matter what your relationship status, remember that positive, close relationships are important for your overall health and wellness. Taking the time to invest in family members and friends is also an investment in your personal health.

Applying the principle of showing love:

Real-life Scenario: It's been a long day at work for both you and your wife. He or she is exhausted and doesn't feel very well. The kids are needing to eat, complete homework and laundry needs to be done as well. **What will be your response to supporting your husband or wife by showing love, if this was your scenario?**

Appropriate responses:

Husband to Wife: Good evening, Beautiful. I am sorry you had such a tough day. Here, let me take your purse and jacket. Why don't you sit here, and I will take off your shoes? Allow me to get you something cold or hot to drink. What would you like, Darling? Sure, here you go, Beautiful. I am going to get your bath water prepared just the way you like it. Don't worry about the kids, I will cook for them and be sure they eat, complete homework and take their baths before bedtime. I will also be sure to complete the laundry. If you have any special items that you would like for me to include, please let me know. I love you, Darling, and is there anything else that you would like for me to do for you? Here, let me help you recline, and I will call you when the bathwater is ready. Afterwards, I will prepare your meal and provide you with bedside service. I will also be glad to massage your tired back and feet. Just relax, it's my pleasure. Hug, Kiss, Kiss. Love you.

Wife to Husband: Good evening, Handsome. I am sorry you had such a tough day. Here, let me take your jacket. Why don't you sit here, and I will take off your shoes? Allow me to get you something cold or hot to drink. What would you like, Darling? Sure, here you go handsome. I am going to get your bath water prepared just the way you like it. Don't worry about the kids, I will be sure they eat, complete homework and take their baths before bedtime. I will also be sure to complete the laundry. If you have any special items that you would like for me to include, please let me know. I love you, Darling, and is there anything else that you would like for me to do for you? Here, let me help you recline, and I will call you when the bathwater is ready. Afterwards, I will prepare your meal and provide you with bedside service. I will also be glad to massage your tired back and feet. Just relax, it's my pleasure. Hug, Kiss, Kiss. Love you.

Inappropriate Response: He or she doesn't speak to each other and bring take-out for themselves without considering each other or the kids. You both go to separate bedrooms and the kids all eat popcorn, pop tarts and ice cream. No one bothers to ensure that the kids' homework is done, and laundry is taken care of. Everyone goes to sleep with TVs blaring, lights on and kids having pillow fights. The kids all pass out asleep throughout the house with no one ensuring they bathe or change into pajamas. The next day, the kids are all late for school or absent because no one ensures that they get to the bus stop on time.

The cycle continues until one day, the couple realizes that they are no longer in love and wants to separate prior to divorcing. Where is the love? Where is the care? What happened to us? These questions are clearly responses after the fact that both spouses have neglected to respond to each other's needs in a responsible manner including the kids. This doesn't have to be your scenario.

Key #2: Respect

Respect is a key that has two phases **(Respect Dreams and The Person)**

Phase 1: Respect Dreams

-      It is important to share and respect each other's dreams by showing support.

-      If they are embarking on a change of career that may require schooling, support him or her in reaching their goals. Celebrate their milestones and achievements while encouraging your spouse to go further.

Phase 2: Respect Your Spouse

-       **Respect the differences that your wife, husband or friend brings to the relationship.** No two people think alike, and opposites attract new ideas that both can discover which may lead to the most beautiful adventure of the relationship. Peanut butter and jelly taste good together even though they are totally opposite of each other. This applies to personalities (one may be an introvert and the other one an extrovert) or (one may be more outgoing while the other partner is quiet or reserved). Your differences should complement the marriage, not disrespect the relationship.

-       **Listen and seek to understand without judging.** Hear each other out and talk instead of shouting your point. Speak calmly and watch your body language. Your non-verbal communication speaks just as loud as your verbal. Have you ever seen a child crying and running away in tears after a parent yell with a facial scowl? Have you ever seen a pet run away and hide after being screamed at? Have you ever been tempted to go to another area of the house or became fearful when your spouse became angry and combative? The brain sends danger alert signals to the body that causes it to take flight or fight which increases anxiety. Want to know the single most powerful step you can take to keep a relationship solid? Speak less and listen more. Blame, insults, criticism and bullying predict a terrible outcome. When the conversation turns combative, don't interrupt, offer a solution or defend yourself too soon. Pause and give your spouse time to complete his or her point. When he or she stops, ask if it's okay to speak. This shows respect for his or her conversation time. It also shows humility on your part. When feelings are involved, they need to be heard. So, nod, rephrase or provide a soft "Um-hum" to show you honor the emotions behind the words. Sometimes, all we really need to do to feel closer to someone is to listen intently to what it is that they're saying.

- Research has also shown that if you speak loving words to a dying flower for a week given it has water, the flower will begin to bloom. The opposite is true if you yelled at a flower for a week. Even if the flower received water, it will die.

I personally like this passage from the Bible, John 1: 1-3, reads: *In the beginning was the Word, and the Word was with God, and the Word was God. The same was in the beginning with God. All things were made by him; and without him was not anything made that was made.* The power of words can create or destroy. I believe this world was spoken into existence by God and if we were created in God's likeness, we must be careful in choosing the words we speak to his creation (i.e., husband or wife). To assist you in choosing your words, I want to provide you with a red-light word selection process that provides a filtering tool for the brain.

- **If you are about to speak something that's not loving, imagine being at a traffic signal**. Use the red-light word selection process by shutting off the signal to your brain that may cause you to use words that could be detrimental to the marriage or relationship.

- I coined this new methodology of psychology as a way of helping others to alter the negative conditioned stimulus of word choice by using traffic signal imagery. Since we are already conditioned to driving using the rules of the road, I thought it would be easier to translate it into imagery that deters bad word choices. The process is simple and here is the method of implementation.

Red Light Image indicates: **Wrong word choice, select another one.**

Yellow Light Image indicates: **Use caution in using this word.**

Green Light image indicates: **Excellent word choice.**

- **It's better to be safe than sorry.** Some words can cause irreparable harm or injury. The heart is fragile and must be handled with care and love.

- **Don't watch TV in the bedroom.** This should be uninterrupted space where you and your spouse focus solely on each other. Now, this may change momentarily as kids are born into the family but overtime, it should return to an area of privacy.

Love is colorblind and has no color. It is irrespective of ethnicity. Don't let others dictate the feelings of your heart. What if you took blood from three individuals from three different ethnicities and placed them into three separate petri dishes to determine their ethnicity. Would you be able to tell? No, and if you were undergoing surgery for a serious injury or accident, would you care whose blood you received? Better yet, if you had heart trouble and needed a heart transplant, would you discriminate in choosing which chest cavity it came from? What about your favorite team, art painting or flavors of ice cream? What if your favorite college or professional team won a championship, would you care about the ethnicity of the person who scored the winning touchdown, set, goalie or basket? If you love ice cream, would you care about the color of the flavor? With these thought-provoking questions, examine your conscious, heart and life. Now, does this evidence tell you why love is a matter of the heart and not ethnicity. If race was the central factor of love, then why are people of the same ethnicity divorcing each other? The truth is the only thing that will set us free if we have been told otherwise. Love from the heart and not from public opinion.

- **Love is not abuse.** *"It is not the bruises on the body that hurt. It is the wounds of the heart and the scars on the mind."* — Aisha Mirza

- As a former police officer, I witnessed many domestic situations where love was not kind but abusive. In cases of abuse, husbands or wives breach their vows when harm is inflicted on the other one. This is in no way a part of the promises made at the altar. This is where the line is crossed and exiting may be the safest alternative to resolve it. Glancing back at the vows, let's review the question:

- *Do you promise to love, honor, cherish and protect him or her, forsaking all others and holding only to her forevermore?* If you include abuse with your actions, you have broken the promise. In this case, you have failed to love, honor, cherish and protect your spouse. This is a violation of civil, criminal, and for believers, God's laws.

- **Research shows that more than 1.5 million women fall victim to domestic violence every year.** However, more than 830,000 men are also victims. Domestic violence is not about size, gender, or strength--it's about abuse, control, and power, and getting out of dangerous situations and getting help, whether you are a woman being abused, or a man.

- **Stop blaming each other for everything that goes wrong.** It's enticing to blame your spouse when you feel angry, discouraged, bored, deceived or tensed about your relationship. Stop viewing your spouse as the one who must change before the relationship gets better. That's an excuse. Blaming your spouse puts him or her on the defensive and projects you in an undesirable light. Furthermore, only spotlighting your spouse for the things that have gone wrong in your relationship means ignoring the 91 percent of him or her that's good and positive. The result? No one changes. No one wants to take responsibility. The relationship sours and becomes unpleasant.

- **Look in the mirror of your own heart**. When you address your own imperfections and seek the best in your companion, great things happen. Optimism grows. Your spouse feels better because he or she feels appreciated, not criticized. And you both feel inspired to change in ways that lead to a more enjoyable relationship.

- **Respect each other by respecting your appearance.** Confess it. You used to complain about your messy hair and fixate over the elegant items to wear to bed. Now, it's dingy sweats and a shabby old T-shirt. Time to fix up your look. Visit a salon or barber, brush those teeth and put on a new wardrobe. When you feel good, look good, and smell good, your spouse will appreciate it and be more attracted to you. The pheromones increase and so does the pleasure.

- **Remain faithful and true to his or her heart.** Love limitless and always.

Applying the principle of showing respect:

Real-life Scenario: It's your spouse's birthday and he or she is excited about celebrating it. He or she awake with hopes of hearing the spouse say, "Happy Birthday." The other spouse leaves for work without a good morning or birthday greeting. **What will be your response to respecting your husband or wife's birthday, if this was your scenario?**

Appropriate responses:

Husband to Wife: He plans a surprise birthday party, months in advance of his spouse's birthday. He rents a limousine, invites her family members along with her favorite friends to come along for the celebration as they travel to a surprise location to celebrate. The day of her birthday finally arrives. "Good Morning and Happy Birthday to the most beautiful woman in the world. Here's a card and some flowers for you, darling. Hug, Kiss, Kiss. Love you." At this point, she goes to work with no clue that the ultimate surprise awaits her later that evening. Both spouses arrive home. He tells her to get dressed for a birthday dinner. They both get dressed and several minutes pass. She gets anxious and suddenly, a chauffeur comes knocking at the door. He answers it. The driver asks for his spouse by name whose birthday is being celebrated. He tells his wife that your driver is here Darling. She looks outside and sees the white stretch limousine awaiting. He then tells her, "let's go celebrate." She is elated but doesn't know that others are inside as she approaches the car. She opens the door, and everyone screams, "Surprise, Happy Birthday!" I share this celebration with you the readers because this is something that I did in showing respect for my wife's 40th birthday. To this day, she still reminisces about that moment, as well as our children.

Wife to Husband: She plans a surprise birthday party, months in advance of his spouse's birthday. She invites his family members along with his favorite friends to come celebrate with her husband. The day of his birthday finally arrived. "Good Morning and Happy Birthday to the most handsome man in the world. Here's a card and a kiss for you, darling. Hug, Kiss, Kiss. Love you." At this point, he goes to work with no clue that the ultimate surprise awaits him later that evening. Both spouses arrive home and she tells him to get dressed for a birthday dinner. They both get dressed and several minutes pass. He gets anxious and suddenly she asks to take him to a dinner location. He agrees, and she drives him to her mother's house. He doesn't understand why they are going there. She tells him that her mother wanted to give him a gift before they went to dinner. He gets out of the car thinking it's a short visit, and his spouse knocks on the door. When the door finally opens the door, everyone screams, "Surprise, Happy Birthday!" I share this celebration with you the readers because this is something that my wife did in showing respect for my birthday. To this day, I still reminisce about that moment.

Inappropriate Response: Simple. Don't give your spouse a birthday greeting, plan something special, provide her with a gift or celebrate him or her. Don't remember their birthday at all.

Key #3: Never Take Each Other for Granted

- **Treat him or her as though it's your last day on earth.** Cherish each moment and spend quality time together. Don't compare apples to oranges if you are starting over. Unpack your baggage at the door and don't dump it off on others. If someone failed you in a relationship, don't take it out on someone else. Move forward with forgiveness and don't stop loving despite the pain. Heal with love instead of reflecting on past hurts or regrets. Seek counseling and appreciate your significant other.

Celebrate your new beginning with pleasure and not pain. I can recall a time that I was conducting ministerial counseling with several persons who were victims of abuse, neglect and abandonment. One was angry and sought revenge. The other was hurt but prayed. And the other party was traumatized and lost trust. In all three cases, I encouraged them to forgive and don't let their circumstances define who they were. After several practices of blocking negative thoughts and experiencing laughter, they healed. All three are now thriving and are doing well in their new relationships. They are being valued and not taken for granted. Nor do they take their spouses for granted.

- **Trust each other, laugh often, love a lot, forgive sincerely.**
- **Give him or her attention by pampering them.** Don't forget to flirt with each other and keep those sparks flying beyond July 4th.
- **Tell him or her how much they are loved and cared for.**
- **Don't text in bed when he or she is seeking your undivided attention.**
- **Don't let arguments turn into a war but put on humility and peace when discussing uncomfortable issues.**
- **Don't belittle or engage in hostile name-calling that tears at the soul and heart of your mate.**
- **Always speak in a controlled loving tone because words have the power to hurt as well as to heal.** Tone says everything and shouting your point tells others that you are out of control.
- **Text or call your partner with messages of love throughout the day.**

- Comfort each other during tough times with encouragement, hugs and advice.
- Compliment his or her hairstyles, clothing, call them by loving, endearing nicknames, and let them know you are on the same team.
- Bring his or her meals and drinks to their bedside.
- Don't text during your mealtime conversations. Your spouse deserves your undivided attention. This also applies to the bedroom or sharing TV moments.
- Put love notes on the car seat, dashboard, inside the lunchbox or windshield.
- Surprise him or her with a celebration.
- Send her flowers or place rose petals on the floor that leads to the bedroom with messages of love on that special Anniversary, Valentine's or Just Because.
- Picnic in the park.
- Carry her to bed when she falls asleep and tucks her in with a kiss on the cheek.

-       **Warm her blanket or towel on those cold nights as she sleeps or gets out of the shower.**

-       **Don't possess your mate, respect them.** If she wants to attend healthy functions with her relatives, female friends or women groups, let her breathe. My wife enjoys meeting with a women's ministry group and on occasions, she will join her relatives in my absence. I enjoy seeing her thrive and share the wonderful experiences of her "Me Time." I stay and have fun with the kids by going to a movie, swimming or just playing games. Remember this, love is not possession. He or she is not your property or slave. He or she is always to be treated with respect and love whether it be privately or publicly in front of family, friends or colleagues. If he wants to golf, hunt or fish with male friends, let him breathe. If you suffocate each other, your relationship will not be able to breathe, and will eventually die. Don't neglect or disrespect each other by taking this to the extreme but keep it balanced. Don't say I didn't warn you if you suffer from insecurity from a past failed relationship or personal issues and your current relationship fails. What went wrong in your childhood, past relationships or family is not your spouse's fault. Unpack your suitcase and throw out the baggage before tying the knot. It's not fair to punish your spouse for something they had no fault in. Marriage is not a prison, it's a relationship.

-    Applying the principle of never take your spouse for granted:

Real-life Scenario: Your spouse becomes gravely ill to the point of hospitalization.

What will be your response to not taking your spouse for granted, if this was your scenario?

Appropriate response: When my wife became seriously ill, I didn't hesitate in seeking medical attention for her. As she was being placed on life support, I asked if I could change her clothes and get her into a gown, which I did. A nurse standing by watched me with tears streaming down her eyes. I completed the task and stood by praying while holding hers and my son's hands. I remained by her side telling her I loved her as she lain in a comatose state. The doctors gently informed that there was nothing more they could do and asked if she was an organ donor. I informed them that I was not ready to accept this as a finale to our journey and decided to continue praying. On the fifth day of her coma, she became responsive and I am very grateful to say that she pulled through with the help of God. Although it was challenging and emotional during this stressful moment of her sickness, I never wavered in my commitment to fulfill my vows of loving her and being supportive through _sickness and in health._ So, if you think marriage is all health, happiness and bliss, you may be disappointed. It comes with laughter and at times there will be some tears. Just remember to laugh and cry together. You are one and it's okay to lean on your spouse for support. Don't take each other for granted. Live in the moment and love them every minute. Tomorrow isn't promised to any of us.

Inappropriate Response: Simple. To give up on your spouse. But please, don't give up on your spouse. It's for better or worse, sickness and in health, for rich or poor. Vows are **not just stated** but **demonstrated** through acts of commitment.

Key #4: Spend Quality Time Together

- It's important to plan monthly date nights.

- Go to movies.

- Attend events as a couple.

- Holding hands while walking together.

- Take time to stare into each other's eyes without turning away. This keeps us focused.

- Cuddle in each other's arms.

- Hold hands while walking.

- Open her car or truck door.

- Always greet and be polite to each other: Good morning, Good night, Thank You, Please, etc.

- If it's raining, go get the car and hold the umbrella to protect her from getting wet as she enters the car.

- Cook meals together and guys it's okay to cook inside as well as outside. The most romantic times are spent in the kitchen.

- **Clean the house together and support each other as you all tidy things up.** Teamwork makes the dream work.
- **Swim or take a stroll in the park together.**
- **Choose a vacation destination and celebrate each other on a cruise or resort island.** Reflect on the memories as you make them.
- **Attend symphonies or concerts together.** Have fun!
- **Help raise the kids and don't leave it all up to her.** I often changed diapers, warmed bottles, picked up toys, cleaned the house and did (and still do!) grocery shopping.
- **Agree to disagree with a compromise where you both can come to a consensus on.** It's not always about whose right or wrong. It's about both parties feeling good about contributing equally toward the best interest of the marriage.
- **Improve your relationship by relaxing and choosing happiness.** The happier your spouse feels, the happier your

relationship will be, and the easier it will be to manage conflicts. Pursue a new hobby to help you relax such as reading, exercising and attending events that are wholesome. Great feelings will lead to happier, loving moments together.

- **Learn to live in the moment of enjoying your spouse and block out negative thoughts.** Avoid allowing bills, financial crisis, unforgiveness and other negative thoughts crowd your mind when you are in a moment with the person you love. It's important to control where your mind wanders. You shouldn't just be with your spouse in body, but your mind should be there too. Your spouse can tell, and he or she usually expresses it by saying, "You are not listening to me." They deserve not just the quantity of time but quality time with you.

- **Applying the principle of spending quality time together:**

Real-life Scenario: Your spouse is complaining about not spending enough time together.

What will be your response to spending quality time with your spouse, if this was your scenario?

Appropriate responses: As a spouse, you should pause, listen, and evaluate the situation. Schedule quality time together such as date nights. Ask your spouse where she would like to go. Be fair in choosing your locations.

Inappropriate Response: Simple. Just ignore their needs. But in all seriousness, don't ignore your spouse's call to spending quality time with you. You don't want to starve or deprive your spouse of quality time. It recharges the relationship and keeps it alive.

Key #5: Reminisce About the Early Years of Dating

-    It's important that you keep your focus on what's important by recalling the memories of love that brought you together. This way the marriage or relationship thrives with happiness. You must water the roses of your love by sprinkling the petals with kindness daily. Reflecting on the positive qualities of your mate is like rekindling a fire. You must keep the bonfire of your heart and relationship burning throughout the journey.

-    **Pick up your wedding photo and quietly reflect before sharing 3 things that you loved about that day as you openly reflect on that day.**

- **If there are ever wonderful children in the marriage, allow them to see you all celebrate each other.** Don't forget that it's important for the father and mother to openly express their love for each other. This will give the children an idea of how a healthy relationship thrives. It's important that they see how you both resolve challenging situations, so they can understand how to resolve conflicts in a respectful but loving manner.

- Applying the principle of reminiscing about the early years of dating:

- **Real-life Scenario:** Your spouse wants to dance to her favorite songs and reminisce about the beginning of your relationship.

- **What will be your response to reminiscing about the early years of dating, if this was your scenario?**

- **Appropriate responses:** Select your favorite love songs and dance together. Every year, I put on my favorite love songs that expresses my love for my spouse such as *Always and Forever* by Heatwave, *Unchained Melody* by The Righteous Brothers, *Through the Years* by Kenny Rogers and *On the Wings of Love* by Jefferey Osbourne. If you don't have a playlist, create one.

- Take her back to the spot where you first met or saw each other. Stand and stare at each other while telling how you felt about when you first laid eyes on each at that location. This helps to reset and restart afresh with the same fire you began with. I even celebrated our 15th wedding anniversary at the same spot where I first laid eyes on her. I surprisingly drove her to the college where we both first saw each other. I escorted her to the very same bench she was sitting on and knelt on one knee and began reminiscing about that first encounter. I then provided her with a new wedding ring to mark our milestone of love.

- **Inappropriate Response:** Simple. Ignore the memories that you've shared together and go through life as if marriage is a duty, not a covenant of love. But please, don't ignore your spouse's call to reflect on the memories of how you all came together as a couple. In other words, don't let the candle burn out, and if so, light it again by reminiscing.

- Key #6: Worshipping and Serving Together.
- A family that prays together, stays together. It should never be said that the only time you knelt before God was at the altar of your wedding. You should both should kneel before your God daily.
- You must remember that the altar and church are not just for marriage. It's a place to spiritually bond, worship and begin a spiritual track of wholeness and completeness. Take time to read or study the bible together. Share in the discussion because it enriches communication. Connect with a couples' ministry because this is where you will meet others who will provide insight into helping you all grow spiritually and emotionally in the marriage. Finally, get involved in serving as you worship. Volunteering to serve in the church and community is ideal for learning how to work together in harmony.

- Applying the principle of worshipping and serving together:

- **Real-life Scenario:** Your spouse wants to attend church, worship, pray and serve.

- **What will be your response to worshipping and serving together, if this was your scenario?**

- **Appropriate response:** He or she should be responsive by making it a daily journey to pray, read the bible, worship and serve others throughout the week.

- **Inappropriate response:** I am too tired, busy and see no need to participate. Besides, I just want to fish, watch the game, or relax on my Sundays off.

Just a reminder: God is never too busy or tired for us, Right?

Key #7: Giving Together

- **First, let's look at the definition and purpose of the tithe in the Christian religion.** The main principle behind tithing and giving is the fact that what we do with our money shows where our heart is. Matthew 6:21 reads: *"For where your treasure is, there your heart will be also."* When we can give 10% or more of our income instead of keeping that money for ourselves, it shows that our heart isn't tied to our money and that we love God more. Plus, it's hard to deny that it feels so good to give towards a good cause, no matter who you are, or what you do or don't believe in.

- **Applying the principle of giving together:**

- **Real-life Scenario:** Your spouse wants to give 10% to a local church or charity.

- **What will be your response to giving together, if this was your scenario?**

- **Appropriate response:** Make a commitment to tithe 10% of earnings as a way of demonstrating love for God or to do something that makes the world just a little bit better.

- **Inappropriate response**: "I don't earn enough to give that much away." "I have bills to pay." "This was Old Testament views, it's not necessary anymore." "The church just wants your money." "Shouldn't the government take care of poor people."
- *"Well, then," Jesus said, "give to Caesar what belongs to Caesar, and give to God what belongs to God."*

*** Give and it shall be given unto you. ***

How to Handle Conflicts Within the Relationship

Believe it or not, conflict is very normal and even beneficial to the relationship at times due to various perspectives. What matters is how you deal with conflict and how to resolve it. Research has shown that couples who are able to effectively problem-solve are highly satisfied in other areas of the relationship. This can create a more solid foundation because you can agree to disagree with a compromise that benefits both.

Be sure to stay away from destructive criticism, unrelenting clashes and hateful words. It's like setting off a nuclear bomb. Studies have shown that over time most couples who divorce in the early stages of the marriage are usually engaged in heated arguments and constantly criticizing each other.

Successful and joyful couples avoid giving into confrontational thoughts that may drive to harm their spouse. Instead, when a conflict arises with any type of potential negativity, they change the subject, involve laughter, listen empathetically or show more love. They also delay the discussion, allowing things to calm down before going into the conversation.

I like to refer to it as (**TPRAC**) **Think, Pause, Reflect and Approach with Calmness.** Addressing the issue is the heart of the matter and a muted person can't speak or respond. Neither can a wounded spouse. So, give equal time to both sides of the discussion. Remember to never go to bed angry with your spouse. It's like sleeping on a bed of nails and neither person gets any sleep because of the pounding irritation of an unresolved conflict. Revisit the discussion with humility and take time to hear each other out. Let me help you out by posing a real family crisis scenario.

- Applying the principle of handling conflicts within a relationship:
- **Real-life Scenario:** Your spouse wants to attend a family reunion and you are planning to attend a wedding on the same day. It has been tensed in trying to reach a compromise because neither wants to give.
- **What will be your response in handling this conflict, if this was your scenario?**

-       **Appropriate response:** Both spouses need to think, pause, reflect and approach the situation with calmness before speaking. After adjusting their emotions, both spouses can speak from their hearts. Some questions to pose: How important is the wedding to you? How important is the class reunion to you? Next question: How many days is the family reunion? If the wedding ceremony is the only event you will be attending that day, can you both attend the wedding and pick which days to attend the family reunion? The situation can be resolved with an agreement that both reached a compromise on.

-    **Inappropriate response**: "Well, okay, you go your way and I'll go mine." This is not acceptable and shows selfishness with disrespect. You must understand that common ground is much better than territorial ground. Marriage is not a predator and prey relationship. It's a union of husband and wife, not *Clash of the Titans*. For, according to Amos 3:3 (WBT), *³Can two walk together, except they are agreed?*

What Do Women Need from Men?

There are many things that women need from men in a relationship, but some of the most significant are:

✓ To be admired and cherished.

✓ To be loved and cared for.

✓ To be respected.

✓ To feel supported in all areas of being (i.e. emotional, spiritual, physical, psychological).

✓ To feel attractive.

✓ To feel that love, intimacy and bonding are on a continuum of maturity.

✓ To feel secure in knowing that he is navigating the relationship towards a bright future.

✓ To grow as one in the relationship

✓ To move forward together in establishing plans, goals and dreams for the road ahead.

✓ To be able to trust him, as he trusts her.

✓ To be able to communicate openly without being judged, criticized or ignored.

✓ To be able to enjoy humor and have fun with him.

✓ To be surprised with gifts, cards, vacations, and special moments of celebrating the relationship with her.

✓ To be listened to, heard, and cherished.

✓ To be cuddled, kissed, and massaged from time to time.

✓ To be publicly recognized and appreciated in front of family, friends or guests.

✓ To not be afraid to cry in front of her and communicate his feelings openly.

✓ To be sensitive, yet, assertive to handle business appropriately.

✓ To be able to provide for her (i.e. shelter, finances, transportation, food).

✓ To feel important.

✓   To be able to stare into his eyes with love. It's the little things that goes a long way.

✓   To sit by the fireplace or bonfire together in the wintertime.

✓   To cook and decorate with her.

✓   To share the responsibility of raising the kids with her.

✓   To clean, do laundry and take care of the home with her.

✓   To let the toilet seat down and clean the restroom from time to time.

✓   To feel a sense of safety or protection when danger is lurking nearby.

As you can see from the list above, what a woman really needs is someone who she can rely on, look up to and remain happy to be in love with. However, once everything has settled, it's up to the man to take the relationship from the amusement and infatuation to a deeper, more lasting love and attraction. But what about a man's needs? Isn't it fair to say that his needs are equally important? Sure, it is! And, the list is as follows...***

What Do Men Need from Women?

✓   To be family-centered.

✓   To be polite and kind.

✓   To be intellectually stimulating.

✓   To be caring and sympathetic.

✓   To have dreams and goals.

✓   To be stable and committed.

✓   To be supportive and giving.

✓   To be compatible.

✓   To be personable, adventurous and sociable.

✓   To be humorous and fun.

✓   To be loving and romantic.

✓   To appreciate him for who is and not compare him to others.

✓   To respect him.

✓   To bring out the best in him.

✓   To stand by him when he feels insecure, lonely and afraid.

✓   To be secure in her own identity and what she wants from him.

✓   To be appealing to him. It sends a message that you're still interested in being attractive to him, physically, emotionally, and romantically. *Bonus: men love sweet-smelling perfumes and satin gowns.

✓   To cuddle close every night, smile and stare him in the eyes with love before going to sleep.

✓   To help in the decision-making; especially when it's hard for him to say "no" to the kids.

✓   To be able to kiss his angel good morning before heading out for the day.

✓   To be humble, not combative.

As one can see, every man has his own 'checklist' for what he is looking for in the woman that he would consider the ideal wife to be. Yet, I am sure that most men would agree with me after seeing this list. Under the same token, I'm sure that most men can also agree with the following as well when it comes to what not to do when it comes to women.

What Men Should Never Do to Women

1. Don't make a woman feel unimportant

Despite bills needing to be paid and other necessities to give attention to, it's important that men not place long work hours, hobbies, buddies, and ambitions ahead of the woman. She will begin to feel lonely, neglected, ignored, empty, unloved, devalued, and abandoned. It's okay to provide for your spouse to have a brighter future, but if you neglect her, the relationship will not last. A man must put the woman's needs first, that is, if he wants to have a long and happy relationship. You must do whatever is necessary to make her feel cared for, loved, and wanted. Respect her opinions because she has a voice and yours is not the only one that matters in the relationship. If that was the case, you could have kneeled while looking in a mirror and proposed to yourself. You could have put on a bridal gown, veil and stood at the altar looking in the mirror and exchanged vows and promises to yourself. Better yet, you could have given yourself away and walked down the aisle to meet yourself. During the reception, you could have danced with yourself and your father, placed cake in your mouth for two and drank two glasses of champagne. Oh, I forgot, you could have walked yourself inside as they announced the wedding party and they would have saved time and just called your name. Do you get the picture as to why women are important? It is important to communicate with your woman. No woman wants to feel ignored or abandoned when she's trying to communicate. This is also romantic for a woman as well. It doesn't start in the bedroom; it begins early on in the relationship with understanding and communication.

2. Don't make a woman feel like she has no identity.

Although women love it when you give them genuine attention, care and romance, most women don't enjoy being smothered or oppressed in a relationship to the point where the man is focused compulsively on her.

Naturally, some women in the world love the notion of being with a man who puts her on a pedestal and focus his life around her but that's not going to make the relationship last forever. She will grow weary of a man she can control, or, the man will feel she's not keeping up by giving back in the same way. Now, he will begin to complain about it and frustration sets in causing conflict.

Women want a man with goals, aspirations, and dreams. She needs to be able to look up to him but at the same time be her own person. A man should never dismiss a woman's feedback, idea or reasoning. Joint decision-making is necessary for establishing a healthy relationship. She wants a man who has her back, side, front and feet when a crisis arises. A man should never put her down because she voices a concern, point of view or perspective. She should always be respected and never be forced to compromise her identity to please a dominating man.

I think all women want a man that is self-assured without being egotistical, candid without being hurtful, strong (not just physically strong, but truly emotionally strong), has good values and morals, will make her laugh every moment of every day and bring out her inner child, and always remind her how valuable she is. It's important to respect a woman for who she is and not for what you want her to be. She is her own person besides being your spouse. She is not your child and deserves to be treated like the adult that she is.

3. Never make a woman feel unattractive

Before your woman met you, she spent hours making herself appealing with hopes of meeting the man of her dreams who would make her feel beautiful by staring at her, complimenting her, and giving her the attention she deserved. That man is **You.**

Even though a woman might be beautiful on the outside, for most women, insecurity about their attractiveness is a struggle. So, it's up to the man to continue making a woman feel as though she's as beautiful as the day he met her. Even if she gains weight, dresses more conservatively, starts to gray, or contends with wrinkles and gravity, she's still that beautiful rose! A man must keep *"watering his precious flower"* by flirting with her, loving her, and never stop kissing or caressing her. If he doesn't, the woman will begin to feel unattractive, neglected, insecure and depressed. She will begin to withdraw, lose romantic interest, sad, lonely, unhappy, or she will leave the relationship due to feeling deprived and starved of love. To put it metaphorically, if you don't water the roots of your rose, the petals will begin to wither, crumble, fall and eventually the plant will die.

However, when you really love and cherish your woman and, she loves you no matter how you both change over time physically (e.g. old age, gray hair, weight gain, sickness), the deep sincere love and attraction you both feel only gets strong over time. Instead of seeing her aging as a sign of getting older, choose to see it as a sign of fulfilled vows and promises you both made at the altar. When a woman feels good about herself, age is nothing but a number because her youth still shines inside and outside of her. If you make her feel attractive, she will make you feel the same. There may even be some perks in it. If she's happy, then *everybody is happy,* including the relationship.

Take care of the most precious jewel that God has given you and she will, in turn, take care of you. Always remember this, you don't miss the water until the well runs dry. Have you checked the well of your relationship lately? If not, you better make sure the water of love is still flowing by letting her know she's attractive every day. So, if you don't have a romantic name for your spouse, choose one today before it's too late. As for my wife, I choose to call her simply, "Beautiful, Sweets, or Queen." What romantic name will you choose in letting your woman know she is still attractive to you? If you don't, somebody else will. Don't get jealous, get on the job! If you treat her like trash today, somebody may one day come along and collect her as a treasure. In other words, treat her like the queen that she is and in turn, she will treat you like the king that you are. *Happy wife, Happy Life*!

Now, discussing the next topic that could equally affect the relationship is...

What Women Should Never Do to Men

1. Don't make a man feel unimportant

A woman should never embarrass a man in front of friends, family or colleagues. This is like putting a child with stage fright on a stage for the first time. It is the most uncomfortable and humiliating experience that a man could ever endure. He then wants to run off the stage of the relationship and into a place of safety, far away!

2. Don't belittle him in front of the kids

Anytime a woman belittles her spouse in front of the kids, she strips him of his authority and dismantles his ability to guide and receive respect as an equal party in raising the kids. So, when the kids are not behaving and he's just sitting on the couch appearing stone-faced while they are emptying cornmeal on each other's head in the kitchen, remember he's resigned from disciplining them. Therefore, he tells the kids to go ask their mother anytime they want to do something. He feels he has no power, undermined and doesn't consider the relationship as being classified as a strong, united, binding cord, but instead, as a weak, worn, unraveling thread. Respect him and he will show the kids how to respect. In turn, the kids will give equal respect when they see respect being modeled between the parents. Action speaks louder than words!

3. Never turn your back to your husband

Unless there are times of illness or personal issues, a woman should never turn her back to her husband in anger. A relationship is not about begging for romance. It is supposed to consist of romance. To deprive your husband of romance is to starve his soul, body, spirit and mind. Sooner or later, the relationship suffers from malnutrition due to the lack of nutrients found in romantic love. Therefore, the relationship goes into cardiac arrest and sometimes no one can resuscitate it. A man that receives his mother's touch as a boy usually requires or needs even more from his wife.

Kinds of Romances

1.   **Being there:** As for romance, women ask that men don't make everything *about* intimacy – i.e., don't do favors that you assume will result in romance being done for you. Your good behavior should not be viewed as a means towards a specific end. Romance can't be bought, and by expecting it as a payoff for doing something that pleases your spouse, you turn a potentially romantic encounter into more of a business deal. Being there for her just might be all she needs at that moment.

2.   **Intelligence:** Carry adventure and excitement into the relationship. Challenge your spouse's views and allow your own to be tested as well. Be open to new ideas and thoughts as you make it safe and welcoming for your spouse to engage. Intelligent stimulation keeps relationships dynamic.

3.   **Loyalty:** Companionship and teamwork go along with friendship and create the bond that keeps most long-term relationships progressing. No one realizes

how little energy they might have for romance once children are born, long work hours, illness or disability occur. There will be times when loyal friendship is what both of you need most from each other.

4. **Verbal:** Verbalizing *"I love you"* are three words that can be highly effective. Unfortunately, some individuals feel that verbalizing these three words make them weak and vulnerable. Your spouse, though, deserves to know that you love him or her. If you are not going to say these three words, make sure your spouse feels your love in ways that matter most to him or her. Everyone needs to feel loved.

5. *Adventurous:* Romance that is focused on pleasing your spouse, not just yourself, is what your spouse needs you to provide. Romance should be a fun adventure that allows spouses to enjoy their romantic connection, not just a repetitive action. Hebrews 13:4 AMP reads: *⁴ Marriage is to be held in honor among all [that is, regarded as*

something of great value], and
the marriage bed undefiled

What All Couples Need

Women need men in their lives just as much as men need them. Men should pause and acknowledge a woman's strengths and respect what she brings to their relationship. And when it comes to romantic bonding, women want the same things men want; they might just want them in a different sequence.

1. To Be Loved

When women feel loved, they are confident and open. The arguments dissipate, the romance is plentiful, and their nurturing womanly energy flows throughout our lives.

Not feeling loved is the underlying issue of every argument that spouses have. If the woman is upset that the man is going out with his friends, or she's frustrated about work, or she is only responding to him with short sentences, then it is likely she is not feeling loved. She must be carefully studied to see how her words, actions, and emotions reflect what may be the cause of her not feeling loved.

2. To Be Safe

There is a conflict being waged on women's confidence, romance, and safety from childhood. Because of the negative stereotypical perceptions sent to women, they need to have a safe space where they feel that they can trust their spouse. A woman wants to trust a man's inner strength and that he can handle whatever she brings to him. She wants to feel like you will not criticize her if she asks for something romantic. She wants to know you won't crumble in defeat if she tells you to do things a certain way instead. By creating a safe zone for your woman to open to you emotionally and romantically, you will be giving her a very powerful gift- you allow her to mature within your relationship and heal long-standing emotional damage.

3. To Be Noticed

Women desire to feel like you see, hear and are aware of her emotions. She doesn't want you impacted by her emotions, just observe it. If she feels like you are not noticing her pain, suffering, tears and emotional trauma, she will lose her trust. She may very well be contemplating, "If he doesn't see that I am hurting, when will he notice me? Is this going to last for hours, days, weeks, months or years? How long will I be hurting, and he is not aware of what I'm going through? Maybe I'll have to depend on myself or friends for support instead of him. Life can be lonely even in a relationship or marriage. As a spouse, you must show your spouse that one person will notice her and what she's going through in life. That one man is **You.**

4. To Be Cared for By Each Other

Just as men have the need to protect, women have the innate ability to nurture. Women desire to see men trusting them when they are hurting or experiencing sadness. So, husbands, it's okay to cry in front of your spouse and let her know how you feel. So often, men or women tend to turn to alcohol, drugs, promiscuity and other mind-altering alternatives because they tend to go into isolation instead of relying on their spouse for support. It's unfair for any spouse to abandon or dismiss their partner's despair as if it's not important. You are sending a message that you don't care about them or their feelings. In no way does this signify your commitment to *"Cherish, Love and Take Care"* of the person you pledge your life to at the altar.

I was very grateful that my mother taught me how to care for a woman by caring for her. You see, women, if a man can't treat his mother with respect and care, what do you think he will do for you? Vice versa, if a woman can't respect or care for her father, men, what do you think she will do to you? Now, I do believe if a person is willing to submit to change and be taught, he or she can become a more loving and caring individual. It's never too late to change and remember it comes from the inside more so than the outside. So, if this is an area where you struggle, seek counseling, attend small group couples' classes and marriage seminars or retreats. Don't forget to apply what you have learned when interacting with your spouse.

Women, if you get upset, hostile or frustrated because your spouse opens your car door like a gentleman and take on a feminist combative role such as (e.g. I can close my own door and you don't have to treat me like I'm helpless), you may need counseling. This is a prime example of a hurt, deprived woman who may be carrying a slight resentment towards the male role due to something she lacked from her father or may have seen from her mother. Men, if you refuse to open the car door and never opens it for your spouse, you may need counseling as well. It could be in an indicator that you never saw your father treat your mother with respect or care, or that you may have a slight resentment towards women. This path may seem normal but it's not in retrospect. She is to be treated like the queen that she is and nothing less.

Lastly, if you tend to go into isolation and shut your spouse out when they are trying to help, it leaves the relationship vulnerable. The other spouse may begin to feel like you don't care, trust or accept them. Now, you have two who are suffering in a relationship that is on the verge of *death* and *decay*. An example would be the response of a spouse to the other who would typically rather lean towards denial and angrily yelling, "I'm fine!" when asked what is wrong. This ongoing lack of transparency and humility creates pain in the relationship which leads to ultimate failure in marriages or relationships. So, let your spouse in and allow him or her to love you through it all.

We all need care and someone to love us. Biblically speaking, God didn't take her from a man's back but his rib which puts her beside him symbolically. Genesis 2:18, 21 - 23(KJV) reads:

¹⁸ And the Lord God said, it is not good that the man should be alone; I will make him a help meet for him. ²¹ And the Lord God caused a deep sleep to fall upon Adam, and he slept: and he took one of his ribs and closed the flesh instead thereof; ²² And the rib, which the Lord God had taken from man, made he a woman, and brought her unto the man. ²³ And Adam said, this is now bone of my bones, and flesh of my flesh: she shall be called Woman, because she was taken out of Man.

5. To Be Romantically Desired

When a man or woman romantically desire each other, it is evident in the way they interact. They stare into each other's eyes, use cuddling words, speak politely and engage frequently in activities that promote romantic desires such as watching love stories together, holding hands while taking a stroll, kiss routinely, sip milkshakes from the same container and sleep close together. The obvious contrast between your relationship with your spouse and other relationships is that you have a romantic partner. Women need to feel romantically desired and cherished as feminine beings. Men should always compliment her, touch and hold her lovingly. Let her know she is the most beautiful and romantic woman in the world.

As for men, women should always make eye contact with him and constantly reassure him that he is desired romantically. Men love to be hugged, kissed and cuddled. If a woman isn't affectionate and instead move three miles to the other side of the King- or Queen-Sized bed, it will send a message that she doesn't want to be bothered-- leaving the man feeling isolated and abandoned with additional feelings of loneliness and vulnerability. He then begins to suspect that she doesn't love or desire him romantically. It further leads him to negative thoughts that can pose detrimental to the relationship. Suddenly, he's coming home later, sleeping in other areas of the house, not desiring to go anywhere with his spouse, doesn't want to be touched, angry and frustrated often. If the truth be told, this spells disaster. Women, those of you who have brothers and sons, notice how the boys interact with their moms and daughters with their fathers. The opposite closeness is evident which holds true that from the time we are born, God designed a masterful plan of preparation in allowing fathers to nurture daughters and mothers to nurture sons in preparing them for their future partners. When we go against that natural design, it creates relationship commotions that are outside the realm of God's plan.

My mother raised five boys and nurtured us into being affectionate, loving and caring men. She hugged, kissed and cuddled us. She even allowed us to cry with her when she was sad or hurting. Her act of vulnerability prepared us as men to witness what it meant to be desired. So, we grew up being affectionate and compassionate. She was preparing us for our future brides. So, women, you must prepare your daughters for the grooms. In turn, as men and women, we both have an obligation to love our spouses romantically and love them unconditionally.

Both men and women want to be appreciated with compliments and praises. Always remind your spouse of how much you love, desire and need them. Also, show them rather than tell them. For example, *"I am fully aware of what you mean to me and that you are my world. I appreciate you more than you know. You can count on me through thick and thin. I'll be there whenever you call or need me."* Now doesn't that put a smile on your face? It certainly does mine and it will for your spouse too!

6. To Show Respectful Intimacy

Often in Christian circles, when things start declining in romance and intimacy, someone will refer to 1 Corinthians 7:3-5 (NIV), which says:

³ The husband should fulfill his marital duty to his wife, and likewise the wife to her husband. ⁴ The wife does not have authority over her own body but yields it to her husband. In the same way, the husband does not have authority over his own body but yields it to his wife. ⁵ Do not deprive each other except perhaps by mutual consent and for a time, so that you may devote yourselves to prayer.

God does not ask us to love Him first. He first loved *us*. It's mutual. And romance and intimacy should be mutual, too. This scripture is not to be used as a weapon against men or women. God created it for the marital union between men *and* women. Therefore, when we start saying, "Men need intimacy, and women need to service them," we make romance and intimacy into something very contractional and obligation based. This is where the breakdown begins. Spouses move from enjoying romance and intimacy to tolerating and enduring it.

Are women obligated to have intimacy every time a man wants to? Are we ever allowed to refuse? Well, let's look more closely at this word *deprive*. Deprive suggests that there is a level of intimacy that is necessary for a healthy marriage.

The fact that the preceding verses in 1 Corinthians 7 say that **the husband's body is the wife's, and the wife's body is the husband's,** infers that one person cannot and must not force himself or herself onto the other person. And by force, I'm not talking about just physical coercion. There's emotional blackmail, there's shutting down, there's telling someone, "You're holding back on me, you don't want this marriage anymore, so I have the right to move on".

If her husband's body belongs to her, then she has the right to also say, "I love you, but my body is tired."

If she feels sick or is exhausted, then having ownership of his body also means that she can say, "I just can't right now" without feeling pressured or guilty.

I believe that the context "do not deprive each other" refers to the relationship in its entirety, not individual moments.

So, if, you have regular and frequent intimacy, then, saying, "Not tonight, I'm not feeling well", is not depriving. It simply means *not right now*. Husbands, this is critical when referring to this text. You must make your wife feel desired and respected as a willing participant. Demanding and coercing intimacy is disrespectful and is not acceptable. So, don't use scriptures or any other relationship advice out of context because of your own need to fulfill your selfish desire. Respect the mutual consent of your romantic relationship and she will find you irresistible. Wives, it is also critical that you not punish your husband by depriving him of romance and intimacy when you should be communicating your feelings. This is not mutual, it's unrelated retaliation. Get to the root of the issue and don't use deprivation as a weapon. There is a difference between refusing occasionally and depriving someone habitually. If there are physical limitations, an illness, a crisis that sends the relationship into trauma such as the loss of a child, parent, etc., please be sensitive and respectful.

These are times when the body is in crisis mode and not responsive to romance and intimacy but needs affectionate support through embrace, words and support. I call this *respectful intimacy*. In a time not so long ago, women were treated as property, second-class citizens, handed off from father to husband to brother-in-law or another close relative who could redeem her (if she outlived the husband). How degrading were these times for women! We are not living in those times, yet, why are so many men modeling and wanting to keep these same values around? Guys...it's time to change our ways mentally, not just physically.

What are the Scientific Benefits of Intimacy?

Research has shown scientific evidence of the physiological benefits of intimacy for women. Engaging in romance regularly has the following effects:

1.   Intimacy Increases DHEA— the Hormone that boosts the immune system. It produces healthier skin and decreases depression.

2.   Intimacy Increases Oxytocin—the Hormone that causes the release of endorphins, a natural opiate that relieves pain.

3.   Intimacy Reduces Cortisol—it reduces stress, and thereby reduces cortisol levels which means more balanced blood sugar, blood pressure, and lower acidity in the abdomen.

4.   Intimacy Increases Immunoglobulin A—Antibody which boosts immunity. Women and men who participate in intimacy twice a week have a 30% higher level of immunoglobulin A.

5.   Several studies show evidence that there's increased blood flow with regular intimacy.

6.   Intimacy Increases Life span. In 2014, experts found that women who had regular romance had significantly longer telomeres – boosting their overall life expectancy. This significant finding indicated that romance within long-term relationships has health benefits. Like the plastic tips at the end of shoelaces which stop them fraying, the caps stop DNA from being damaged. Shorter telomeres have been associated with aging, disease, and a higher risk of death. Telomere length is linked to longevity.

What Do Women Need in A Relationship?

But what are a woman's needs and wants when it comes to old-fashioned dating? Women generally want a relationship where their spouses have integrity, strong work ethics, and empathy. They don't want someone who presents himself as a dominating dictator, i.e. *the king of his domain*. However, they do want someone who has the courage to cry in front of her when needed, face his fears, and stand on his own two feet during a battle. Women want someone who is willing to step up and not hide from problems or challenges when they arrive but take charge to protect his family at all costs.

Women enjoy laughter and a positive attitude. No woman wants a grouchy, negative or critical man. It's important for a man to wear a smile and is not ashamed to have wild, childlike fun and laughter. Women want a man they can share ups and downs, highs and lows, dreams and failures, and fantasies with – but leaving out emotional baggage, when wisdom prohibits it. Some things are better left unsaid or shared. Women want a spouse they can confide in without the fear of being criticized. They want a man who is open to new ideas, experiences and positive thoughts.

21st Century women want a confident man who can appreciate an independent woman and admire her strength as a professional, entrepreneur, and responsible mother, while at the same time, admiring that little girl in her anxiously waiting to have fun! They want a man who will be strong, honest without being hurtful, loyal in times of disagreements but able to support her.

Additional things women want in a relationship:

1. An Instinctive Bond

Being bonded can mean different things at different times. It's physical. It's emotional. It's psychological. When you combine all three aspects, you reach a level of bonding that is awe-inspiring. You don't need to be in the same room to feel that bonding. Yet, when you *are* near one another, the energy between you two is strong and cohesive. You become bonded, in every way. From eyeing her across the room to holding her close, your love becomes super-charged and the bond is unbreakable.

2. Signs of Insecurity

Does she *really* need to know? For sure! She needs to be secure about your intentions, or the lack thereof. What do you intend to happen in the relationship? Do you have an ulterior motive up your sleeve? Do you want to see where the chips fall? Or, do you want something more solid? Do you see marrying her in the future or is it just a fling? Whatever it may be, she wants to know so that she isn't wasting her attention on someone or *something* that isn't even going to develop beyond infatuation. **Assurance** and **security** are often interchangeable in a woman's head for the simple reason that they both work in direct correlation of each other. There is no *security* if there isn't any *assurance* and vice versa.

3. Decisiveness of Thought

Assurance translates to decisiveness, eventually. If you're assured about someone or something, you'll be decisive about it in your thoughts, words and actions. Simply put, it will manifest into action. Being decisive is about understanding the value of the person in your life and deciding to show them how much you value them.

4. Willing to Act

Which brings me to my next point—acting on that decisiveness. Many times, in relationships, men are not willing to act—on desire, nature, passion; call it whatever you want. And it is this failure to act that is one of the main reasons why men have something called 'almost relationships' today. Either out of sheer convenience, availability of options, or fear of rejection, we often choose not to act on a feeling; even if at that moment, it may seem like the right thing to do. Soon the moment passes, and with it, the will to act. In relationships, actions always speak louder than words; even though most times, words are just as, if not more, required. And there needs to be a connection between *what you say* and your actual behavior. You can't do one thing and then, say something completely contrary. Confusion leads to uncertainty. This ultimately leads to an unwillingness to act. So, women are looking for a willing partner who isn't afraid to act on his true feelings of showing her love instead of just speaking it. In other words, be willing to take that first step in proposing.

5. Consistent Communication

Humans are communicators, each one of us. We may have different means of communication— some talk, others listen, yet others find ways to communicate without really saying much. Women love men whom aren't afraid to communicate and listen to them. They don't care much about men whom are afraid to share their feelings or discuss issues they feel are important. Please, men, it's important to communicate and express your feelings during the window of opportunity. While relationships and connections are all about the timing in two people's lives, it doesn't take too long for that time to pass you by. Then, sadly, you're left crying with regret because of lost opportunity. Communication is the difference between **'What if'** and **'Yes'**! Don't let love slip away when you had it right in your hand. Women want a man that they can talk to instead of trying to figure him out, like a difficult puzzle. She needs consistent communication, both verbally and non-verbally as well as romance. This goes to the heart of kissing, touching and flirting with her. It's also communication and failing to do so can lead to catastrophic outcomes in the relationship. Whether you know it or not, we speak with not only our mouths, but with our eyes, minds, body, and, especially, our hearts.

Why Men Pull Away from Women

Most women experience anxiety, fear and insecurity when her man begins to pull away and withdraw. Maybe it happens unexpectantly, incidentally, or purposely. Yet, either way, it's a terrible feeling and elevates to where a woman is left feeling helpless and agonizingly uncertain. Questions arise such as: What's wrong with him? Why is he acting this way? What did I do to cause this? Who did this? Who is he seeing? What's wrong with *me*? How can I get through to him? Why isn't talking to me? Why won't he look at me? Why won't he touch me? Why won't he call or text me anymore? Why is he doing this?

You may have asked one or two of these questions in your life while being in relationships. Now the obvious answer is **every man is different and so are relationships**. But here are some general reasons that men pull away or withdraw in relationships:

1. Anxiety

It's no myth that most men isolate themselves in another room of the house with a remote control or hobby when they are extremely stressed. However, there is a contrast between *perceiving* something and being empathetic. Most women struggle to understand that this is how men deal with issues because when they are experiencing anxiety, men would rather talk about it with friends and loved ones to avoid putting pressure on the relationship. He pulls back and withdraws to strategically think and navigate through the crisis. The monumental mistake that women can make is not giving him time to do this. If a woman consistently and insistently coerces him to discuss the issue or talk, he will see her as another source of anxiety and withdraw even more. It's like a tug-a-war of pushing and pulling away. It's important to remember that coercion isn't effective in getting someone to conversate when they are struggling emotionally. You can invite a man to discuss the issue but it's not effective to coerce him into revealing his pain.

When he does decide to discuss the issue, just listen and don't voice your opinions and try to solve it for him. The last thing he needs during this time is criticism which drives him into further depression which could lead to pushing him over the edge causing him further harm. He will ask for your advice if he needs it. Don't pry him. Let it flow naturally and hug him while holding his hand. This lets him know that you're merely there as support and you're aware of his pain.

Remember that men are wired differently than women and no one likes to be coerced. It violates our zones of proximity safety and hinges on the appearance of being disrespectful. Never demand, give space and a man usually steps back towards you. Just like boys do to their mothers, men do the same to their wives. Because stereotypically speaking, societal images indicate that men are supposed to portray this macho image of toughness and it goes against his nature to show vulnerability.

If a man feels like you have an ulterior motive and you're trying to coerce him into a relationship, most of the time his defenses will become triggered. It's not a cognizant choice on his part, but his nature will compel him to pull away, that you're not "the right one," that you are attempting to take his freedom away. Suddenly, he will put up a wall and abort connecting with you on an emotional level. A man immediately puts his guard up when he feels like a woman is trying to get something out of him, it's almost like he's under attack. Therefore, you'll notice he emotionally withdraws and goes cold. At that point, love can't develop, and it basically kills the relationship.

2. He Feels Smothered

Men don't always share personal problems or issues as freely as women. Sometimes too much suffocation from you is enough to cause him to pull away. If a man thinks you *need* him to feel confident in your life, or that you need him to fill an emotional void, he will unconsciously pull back. Men want to feel *desired and needed*, not *smothered*. This is a very important distinction that most women overlook. This doesn't apply to those that are suffering from a debilitating or extended illness. Men are supposed to be there regardless. However, men do love being in relationships, but they fear losing their freedom and getting ensnared in a situation with a woman who drains them dry and leaves them feeling weak and dull. A man will feel *free* in a relationship when he's with a woman who is fulfilled in her life and doesn't depend on the partnership to meet her every want.

If you start to act destitute, it will send a message that he's losing his freedom and he will automatically pull away from you. To repair the damage, simply allow him space and time to focus on you instead of his problems or issues. He will come back every time. In other words, don't force love, allow it to happen freely. Take the strain out of it and relax in confidence. He will feel it and turn to you for resolve. Here's a secret that I want to share with you ladies who are reading this and feeling desperate to pull your man back. Apologize and ask for forgiveness if you feel your tactics have been pushy. Let him know that you're there if he needs you. Kim him, stare into his eyes and hug him. Now, give him space and he will continue to feel your love in his quiet space.

3. Men are Skeptical

Every man gets cold feet when it comes to a long-term relationship. It has nothing to do with you as a woman, he may be reluctant to go any deeper due to his past experiences or childhood. This is the norm for any relationship that men see as serious and long-term. Don't take it personally if he appears cold, fearful and shies away from engagement or marriage. He is just processing it and wondering if he's going to live up to your expectations. That's perfectly okay because couples can be in love but not right for each other in the long haul. Maybe he's having a hard time with commitment and lacks trust. On the other hand, skepticism could be the result of an argument, jealousy, or trauma from a past relationship. Just give him time and space. Just keep being the best you can be as his partner. It doesn't hurt to pray for him and with him if he allows it. Before marrying my wife, I can recall her inviting me to her church, praying with me and reading the bible alongside me. As a man, I couldn't have asked for a better partner than a prayer partner. To encourage your heart, if a man decides to leave after all that you have done, don't bombard yourself with anxiety or regrets. No relationship can work without partners being committed to making it work. Sometimes, he may not be the right person for you. It doesn't matter why your partner is withdrawing, it's important to give him space to work through his issues.

Why Women Pull Away from Men

You're dating a woman and it seems like things are going great until suddenly she stops texting you to ask how your day went, she's not initiating outings like she once did, and when you are together she's looking at her phone or only half-interested in the conversation. Men and women both distance themselves from relationships for many reasons, and when you feel disconnected from someone it can be hard to figure out what's going on.

Imagine you are on a date with the most gorgeous woman in the world. You can't stop holding hands, kissing and staring at each other. When the evening ends, you can't stop calling, texting or face-timing your new love. She is gentle, kind, polite and suddenly everything comes to a halt. One day, you look at your phone expecting to receive a text, call or facetime message. You finally reach her, and she is silent with nothing much to add to the conversation. As you can see, men and women both abandon relationships for various reasons. It's hard to decipher what's happening in situations like this. Men, *if you're concerned about why your woman is pulling away*, it may be just what you are thinking. And it may not be anything to be worried about. Here are some mutual reasons women pull away from a man even when she's in love:

1. Women want men to commit

A woman may be in love with a man and want to spend the rest of her life with him. But the moment, she asks the question (Are you ready for a commitment?) and he fails to answer, she will begin to pull away from him. She may want to be in an exclusive relationship and the man doesn't. At that point, she will begin to fade out by not communicating, texting, face timing and dating. Men must realize that very few women will remain in a stagnant stage of a relationship. If you really love and adore her, take a chance and commit.

2. Women are in love with someone new

Most women pull away from men because they have bonded with another partner. It may have happened by chance and unexpectantly. She may be struggling with her attraction to the other man. There's not much a man can do about this situation other than to hope he can win her over.

Women have a hard time telling a man that she's in love with someone new out of protection for his feelings. They would rather phase out slowly and allow the rest of the flames to smother.

3. Women may realize they are too aggressive

When women fall in love with the person of their dreams, they may be too aggressive in their early approach. To some degree, they may decide to dial things back and slow the pace of the relationship. Most women will pull back and away if they sense the aggression is too much for their partners.

4. Men won't express their emotions.

Women are tolerant of men to a certain extent of allowing him to deal with his emotions but don't want a man who is afraid to express his emotions. After a while, women will get tired of being alone and waiting for men to speak openly. They too will begin to pull away from trying to get through the emotional barriers of men. It's difficult for a woman to accept this kind of rejection when she's doing all she can to be accepted. It's okay for men to share their emotions with women. It brings them closer to your true heart and builds a deeper connection. Don't push her away, pull her to you before she pulls away.

5. Women don't see a future with you.

If you think of speed dating, it is an opportunity for men and women to see if there's chemistry before pursuing the next level of the relationship. Women who are seeking compatible men, waste time by hanging around to see if it's going to blossom. They may not like what they see in certain men after meeting them. As they say, *first impression is a lasting impression.* If a man says he is interested but doesn't call you, that's a red flag. It shows her that you really don't care enough to reach out and this turns women off. Women don't see a future in waiting around for men to make good on their promises. They pull away quickly to avoid dragging it out.

6. A woman lacks love and care.

Women need love, care, kindness, gentleness and attention. If men don't provide these, she will pull away from emotional neglect and move forward. Women function on the connection hormone known as *Oxytocin* which is activated by love and care. If she is void of this connection, she pulls away.

7. We feel emotionally attached too soon.

Women will sometimes feel they are becoming emotionally attached to men too soon. They will pull away thinking it's too much. This is where men must assure women that it's okay and establish calm. Let her know that you understand and it's okay for her to take her time. This will make women fall in love even deeper when they see men helping them take control of their emotions. It shows that men are in tune and aware of women's emotions. This is a plus for the relationship and may prevent her from pulling back even further. Women will feel that they can trust men with their emotions and future.

8. Women often feel neglected.

Research has shown that 80 percent of women who engaged in affairs experienced extreme neglect prior to becoming unfaithful. If men are too busy with other things aside from their relationship and devote little to no time to their women, the result is infidelity or divorce. It's the simple things that keep a relationship alive. It's extremely important for men to compliment, cuddle and show love to women. It could make the difference between women staying or leaving.

9. Women are bored.

Women want adventure, fun, spontaneous trips, romantic intimacy, laughter and surprise celebrations from men. They hate listening to other women talk about their travels and adventures without anything to add value to their relationship with men. If women feel that the relationship has come to a boring standstill or halt, they are going to get off at the next train station or port. Can you blame them? No woman want to watch the reruns of sitcoms every Friday night while men sleep, snore and sneezes so loud the drapes fall every 10 minutes. Women will sense stagnation and boredom. They will bail out and pull away as fast as they came. Men, be sure to add some sparks to your relationship and don't let the fire go out. Women deserve excitement and adventure, not boredom.

10. Women often feel men want intimacy only, not love or affection.

Women want men to want her for more than intimacy. This is disrespectful to women and they feel used. Women need men in their lives throughout the day. Before leaving for work, give her a kiss, say good morning, and tell her that you're looking forward to seeing her soon. During your lunch break, call or text her a compliment. After work, stop by and pick up some flowers or a gift to show your love. When you arrive home, give her a kiss and cook dinner instead of her. Spend time with her and the kids. Just before bedtime, turn the covers back for her and run her bath water for her. Give her a back, leg or foot massage. This is love and affection in action not just spoken. Men, women need to feel like your girlfriend every day and that you never lost sight of her as your woman. If you do lose sight, you will lose her when it comes to intimacy because she's going to pull away.

11. Women have experienced problems in prior relationships and growing up.

Women who have experienced abusive prior relationships or childhood traumas may exhibit a heightened sense of fear, uncertainty and nervousness if men raise their voice, show frustration or cause her to feel threatened. The trauma of failed, neglectful and abusive relationships from the past may have left them in a guarded posture. This is where men must show sensitivity and never rush intimacy. It's important to listen, love, care, and allow women to feel comfortable in trusting the relationship. Never judge or criticize women who have suffered such fates, men are only adding to the trauma and activating triggers causing extreme anxiety. This could lead to emotional setbacks and health problems. So, men should remember to be gentle and handle abused women with care because they are fragile. The least bit of trauma can cause them to break down and pull away. Love her tender and love her sweet. Women should be treated like a rose and nurtured back to health where others failed to do so. Take the time to pray and read the bible with her. This can add to the healing besides the love you as a man will give.

12. Women feel suffocated in the relationship.

Even though women love romance and intimacy, they don't want to be suffocated to the point of fatal attraction. Men could cause women to pull away just to get some space. If women pull away too much, it's fine for men to ask if they are alright. Just don't badger or force them, women just need space and time. Women often enjoy *"Me Time"* or time with her lady friends. If women want to go in their bedrooms and close the door for some quiet time, let them rest in their own space. At least, they're still home. Don't suffocate women, let them breathe the fresh air of the relationship by enjoying her space at times.

What Should I Do If My Spouse Becomes Chronically or Terminally ill?

So often a couple may contemplate this question--*Will he or she stand by me if I become chronically or terminally ill?* Although it is a question that many try to avoid, it is pertinent that it is not ignored. As for my 32 years of marriage, I was faced with this question after my wife became ill. Here's a statement that I would strongly like to make. **Remain committed to your wife or husband.** This is how I did it. I relied on my faith, prayers, support and vow to love her *in sickness and in health*. Love is enduring. It surpasses the temporal and physical and remains strong through the emotional and spiritual. When health declines and bodies age in our loved ones, our faith, patience, and understanding are key. Don't let your emotions control you, let your commitment guide you. If you find your emotions getting in the way, here are some tools for you when facing this crisis. *Hats off to each of you who are currently going through any kind of health crisis with your spouse. I stand in prayer with you.

❖ Get up each day and be thankful for the gift of love that is in your life.

❖ Kiss him or her every day.

❖ Communicate, laugh and smile each day.

Ask yourself this question: "If I were in the same situation, how would I want to be treated?" Here's a practical exercise for anyone facing this challenge.

1. Go and sit beside your spouse.
2. Hold his or her hand.
3. Speak to them gently.
4. Lovingly state: "I am committed to standing beside you through sickness and health. I love and cherish you always. I promise that we will get through this together."
5. Give him or her a hug with a kiss or squeeze and kiss their hand. (If your spouse is unconscious or seriously ill, kiss him or her while visualizing them hugging and kissing you back.)

1 Corinthians 13:4-5, 7 (NIV): "Love is patient, love is kind… It does not dishonor others, it is not self-seeking…. It always protects, always trusts, always hopes, always perseveres. Love never fails."

A Glimpse at International Marriages

Have you ever wondered what other marriages are like in other countries? Let's look at a few countries. Some marriages are very sweet, and others are a bit strange. In Sweden, the wedding guest kisses the bride or groom each time their spouse leaves the reception area. The men will kiss the bride and the ladies will kiss the groom. In China, the bride cries for one hour each day for a month. The bride is joined by her mother and grandmother as they also express emotions alongside her. This is an expression of joy and they also sing as well. In the Philippines, the bride and groom release white doves after the wedding to represent a harmonious life. In Cuba, every man who dances with the bride must pin money on her dress to assist the couple in paying for their wedding. In Italy, the groom throws a surprise party outside the bride's window the night before the wedding. The groom serenades his bride with live musicians playing behind him. But what is unique and binds all these customs both domestic and foreign is one simple theme: *Love.*

Dating

The courtship of any marriage starts with dating before a proposal. Some people meet in various places or under unexpected conditions. Others are still waiting for that Mr. or Ms. Right to come along. Meanwhile, there are some who are starting over after a divorce, death of a spouse, or just deciding to rekindle the sparks of the marriage. Whatever the case may be, it's important to get to know yourself and heal from certain bad situations we all go through in life if you're starting over or beginning to date. If you're looking to rekindle your marriage or relationship, it's important to start by surprising your spouse or partner with gifts such as candy bars with notes attached, roses, cards, notes in her lunchbox, love texts, surprise candlelit dinners, massages or surprise romantic trips. If you're wondering about the dating scenes, remember they vary throughout the world.

America

The dating scene in America varies from meeting others through friends, websites, coffee shops, family, bars, church, apps, gyms or at work. First dates are often relaxed and getting to know the person. Afterwards, if interested, other dates will follow.

China

In China, there are 33.6 million more men than women and there are dating schools for men. If a person is single, elders will usually set them up on blind dates. Speed dating has become popular as well.

United Kingdom

In the UK, the dating scene is like the US with some differences. The British dates are more relaxed, and romance is common early in the relationship as a norm.

Japan

If you're looking for a date in Japan, most people seek someone they can marry. Normally, one single person will invite a group of single friends and another person will do the same for dinner. They will enjoy an evening together and exchange numbers after dinner.

France

In France, the word "date" is non-existent. They prefer to use "I'm seeing someone" meaning they are committed as opposed to dating them. The French are very relaxed and generally indicates that.

Spain

In Spain, they are much like the French and use the verb "salir con alguien" meaning "to go out with someone." Most people in Spain live with parents until married. You are not able to meet the family unless the relationship is getting serious. If you do have the opportunity of meeting the family, it will be the entire family.

Sweden

If you're looking to date in Sweden, you may be disappointed because it's the hardest place to find a partner or establish a relationship. The culture promotes remaining single and the best way to be successful at dating is to be casual. The Swedes enjoy coffee and conversation as opposed to dinners. They also prefer to hug instead of kissing on a date. If you began dating someone by chance, it is assumed that you are exclusive to that person despite how casual it is.

Mexico

In Mexico, dating is more traditional. Men are expected to approach the women first, pay for their meals and pursue future dates. Mexicans are affectionate and often hug and kiss in public.

United Arab Emirates

In the United Arab Emirates, you are not allowed to show affection in public or engage in romance before marriage. It doesn't mean that it doesn't occur. However, most of the population are foreigners. This makes it simple to meet, conversate and ask others out for a date. Men are customarily the ones to ask the women and pay. Dates normally occur in bars, movies or indoor skiing arenas.

India

In India, dating is usually permitted with the approval of family members since most of the country still believes in arranged marriages. This means that the family usually decides on who their son or daughter will date prior to marriage. Getting in a relationship usually means that one is intending to marry. However, there is some evidence that things are changing with technology allowing others to meet via websites.

Italy

In Italy, romance is key to dating. Romance is casual and a norm earlier on the dating process.

Brazil

In Brazil, dating is serious and normally leads to marriage in a relatively short period of meeting one another.

However, dating traditions and customs all begin with relationship building. This is essential for all couples who are seeking to build or restore a connection to growing with a spouse. Without a relationship, there is no date, just a temporary notion. Whether you're starting over or beginning, it's important that you understand your spouse or partner before pursuing the next step. Getting to know, love and understand the person is about rekindling the flames of the heart.

Accepting Forgiveness

It's easier to hold a grudge than to let it go. This is where relationships get tense because some spouses or partners are in the revenge mode and have a hard time accepting forgiveness. They must find a way to get justice, so they resort to some of the most violent creative retaliatory tactics such as *(i.e., keying the car, slashing tires, shattering car windows, burning the car, burning clothes, burning the house, imposing physical harm, infidelity, spreading false harmful rumors, sabotaging employment, contacting tv shows, filing civil suits, resentment, hate, filing false police reports, recruiting friends and family members to assist in retaliation).* Always remember this, two wrongs don't make a right. This is the toughest part for those who have been wounded. Let me share a story that may help open your heart to accepting forgiveness. Many years ago, during the 1960s, the Late Alabama Governor, George Wallace, ordered police to inflict pain on African Americans who marched for civil rights in Montgomery, Alabama as they marched to Selma. Some suffered dog bites, beatings, unlawful arrests, tear gas, and hate at the hands of police. If you know George Wallace's story, you know that he retracted his racist views of hate and asked forgiveness from African Americans 30 years later. At the age of 75 and in a wheelchair, Governor Wallace was too ill to make a speech to the 200 marchers, largely African Americans, who gathered at the St. Jude School in Montgomery, as they did three decades ago. His aide read his remarks as Mr. Wallace, almost completely deaf, sat in silence. "Much has transpired since those days. A great deal has been lost and a great deal has been gained, and here we are. My message to you today is, "Welcome to Montgomery." Some argue about the motive behind change-of-heart. Some didn't believe him. Some wouldn't believe him. Others wouldn't forgive but a few did forgive him. I say, whatever starts that step toward change — embrace it. Accept it. According to a 1995 Baltimore Suns article, The SCLC President, Rev. Joseph E. Lowery remarked to Governor Wallace: *"Thank you, for coming out of your sickness to meet us. You are a different George Wallace today. We both serve a God who can make the desert bloom. We ask God's blessing on you."* What an act of accepting forgiveness.

Unforgiveness is a prison but forgiveness frees the soul. So, accept forgiveness from your spouse, fiancé or fiancée and remember, it's about releasing yourself from the pain. Don't hold your marriage or relationship hostage if the situation calls for accepting forgiveness. Let go of your retaliatory and vengeful attitudes. Love one another because life is too short and you don't want to waste it living hate, do you?

Til Death, we will never depart.

In conclusion, I offer this prayer of unity and hope for all relationships. I hope you will say it throughout the journey of your relationship and into marriage. Let us pray: "God, You are our source of strength, provision and protection. I ask that You bless this unity of my spouse and I as we journey down life's pathway. Be a lamp to our relationship as Your word is a lamp to our feet. Place Your hedge of protection around us and keep this relationship grounded in love, respect, care, unity, trust and You. We give You thanks for bringing us together and with Your guidance, our prayer is that You keep us together as we grow as one. To You, the One God that is above all, we thank You for hearing this prayer. Amen.

A Poem Written for My Wife

Your Eyes

Your breathtaking beauty
Shined right through me
As I stared into your eyes

Captivated by your smile
You caught me by surprise
My feelings, I no longer disguised

The moment I held you
in my arms
I knew you were the one for me
Our hearts began beating
As one
It was clear we were meant to be

As I knelt before you
on bended knee
I asked for your lovely hand
With this ring of promise
You gladly accepted
Me as your devoted man

FLAMING TIMBERS

Couples & Singles Enrichment Retreats

Thank you for reading and check out Flaming Timbers' Couples and Singles Retreat at https://www.flamingtimbers.com/

ABOUT THE AUTHOR

Dr. Fletcher Johnson Jr. is an author, counselor, and educator. He has been married 32 years to his wife, Valerie, and together they have three sons, Jarvis, Christopher, and Joshua. He firmly believes that even though no one's perfect, all couples still wield the power to create an ever-lasting relationship filled with passion and love.

References

Anon, (2019). *If He's Pulling Away, Do This….* [online] Available at: https://www.anewmode.com/what-to-do-if-hes-pulling-away/7/?L=26805 [Accessed 6 Jul. 2019].

Bourgeois, T. (2017). *What George Wallace Taught Me About Forgiveness*. [online] Huffpost.com. Available at: https://www.huffpost.com/entry/what-george-wallace-taugh_b_6647468?guccounter=1 [Accessed 6 Jul. 2019].

Bragg, R. (1995). *Baltimore Sun – 30 Years Later, Wallace Apologizes to Marchers*. [online] Baltimoresun.com. Available at: https://www.baltimoresun.com/news/bs-xpm-1995-03-11-1995070104-story.html [Accessed 6 Jul. 2019].

Bruns, T. (2019). *What Do Women Want in a Relationship? |Marriage.com*. [online] Best Marriage Advice - Get Marriage Tips from Experts. Available at: https://www.marriage.com/advice/relationship/wha

t-do-women-want-in-a-relationship/ [Accessed 6 Jul. 2019].

Gregoire, S. (2019). *What Does 1 Corinthians 7:5–Do Not Deprive Each Other–Really Mean? | To Love, Honor and Vacuum*. [online] Tolovehonorandvacuum.com. Available at: https://tolovehonorandvacuum.com/2012/10/what-does-1-corinthians-7-do-not-deprive-each-other-really-mean/ [Accessed 6 Jul. 2019].

Hendrix, S. (2018). *Here's what dating is like in 20 countries around the world*. [online] INSIDER. Available at: https://www.insider.com/what-dating-is-like-in-different-countries-2018-5#the-topic-of-marriage-comes-up-quickly-in-ugandan-relationships-20 [Accessed 16 Jul. 2019].

Marie Hartwell-Walker, E. (2019). *Stages of Marriage*. [online] Psych Central. Available at: https://psychcentral.com/lib/stages-of-marriage/ [Accessed 6 Jul. 2019].

Mattia, N. and Park, A. (2019). *47 Fascinating Wedding Traditions from Around the World*. [online] brides. Available at: https://www.brides.com/gallery/wedding-traditions-around-the-world [Accessed 15 Jul. 2019].

McDermott, N. (2017). *How Having Sex Will Help You Live Longer*. [online] whimn. Available at: https://www.whimn.com.au/love/intimacy/have-lots-of-sex-and-youll-be-around-for-a-lot-longer/news-story/658e83a24776833d079a1de66a28cacc [Accessed 6 Jul. 2019].

Officiant Eric. (2019). *Exchange of Wedding Rings*. [online] Available at: https://www.officianteric.com/exchange-of-wedding-rings/ [Accessed 6 Jul. 2019].

Papa, A. (2018). *Why Women Pull Away and What You Can Do*. [online] The Date Mix. Available at: https://www.zoosk.com/date-mix/relationship-advice/why-women-pull-away/ [Accessed 6 Jul. 2019].

Ponti, A. (2019). *Why Men Pull Away: 5 Reasons Why & How To Make It Stop!*. [online] Apollonia Ponti. Available at: https://www.apolloniaponti.com/why-men-pull-away/ [Accessed 6 Jul. 2019].

Reader's Digest. (2019). *The 7 Stages of Marriage*. [online] Available at: https://www.readersdigest.ca/health/relationships/7-stages-marriage/ [Accessed 6 Jul. 2019].

Some Religions More Likely to Divorce, According to Study. (2019). Retrieved 18 July 2019, from https://www.wevorce.com/blog/what-faith-divorces-most/

Sutton-Deangelico, T. (2019). *10 Things You Should Tell Your Spouse Every Day for a Happier Marriage*. [online] Reader's Digest. Available at: https://www.readersdigest.ca/health/relationships/marriage-advice-things-say-spouse/ [Accessed 6 Jul. 2019].

www.ingramcontent.com/pod-product-compliance
Lightning Source LLC
Chambersburg PA
CBHW050129280326
41933CB00010B/1312